THE SIBERIAN SHAMAN
IN WESTERN MYTH

Other Works by Sandy Krolick

Вероника: Сибирская Сказка (Novel)
VERONIKA: The Siberian's Tale (Novel)
The Recovery of Ecstasy:
    Notebooks from Siberia
Apocalypse of the Barbarians:
    Inquisitions on Empire
Conversations On A Country Path
Gandhi in the Postmodern Age
Recollective Resolve
Ethical Decision-making Styles
Культурныи критицизм
Myth, Mystery and Magic:
    Religious Imagination in Ancient Egypt
Russian Soul and Collapse of the West
Shambhala (Novel)
Misha (Novel)
On Being and Being Good
Q: Interpreting QAnon
A New Heaven and a New Earth
Philosophic Play On Culture and Society
Babel Unhinged:
    Collected Essays in Philosophical
    Anthropology and Cultural Criticism

THE SIBERIAN SHAMAN
IN WESTERN MYTH

sandy krolick, ph.d.

Islands Press

New York : Altai Krai

ISBN: 978-1-7350698-7-6

Cover art courtesy of:
Yuri Ivanov
Altai Krai, Russia

THE SIBERIAN SHAMAN
IN WESTERN MYTH

Prelude

YOU may not know this, but January 6, 2021, was not the first outing of a shaman within our midst. Nor, most likely, will it be the last. Perhaps what follows will provide some background and historical context on the important place that shamanism has occupied within our world and, not in the least, in our storied wintery mythology. But let's first change gears by investigating the primitive and pre-historic roots of our topic before I spill the beans too early.

Introduction

SINCE the early twentieth century ethnologists and anthropologists have frequently used the words 'shaman,' 'sorcerer,' 'medicine man' and 'witch-doctor' interchangeably. Such terms have ordinarily been applied to those persons within pre-urban or 'primitive' societies who possess magical or special healing powers. In fact, the term 'shaman' has been used to describe much the same phenomenon among civilized peoples as well. There is, for example, Babylonian, Indian, German and Chinese shamanism, among others. In fact, remains of a female shaman dating back more than eight thousand years have recently been recovered from an archeological excavation of hunter-gatherers in the area of Bad Dürrenberg, Germany.

BUT shamanism has become a New Age phenomenon in America, challenging Buddhism as the hot spiritual practice of today. Witness the halting presence of the QAnon shaman leading the breach of our nation's Capitol in January of 2021. BE that as it may, shamanism can be a tricky term to pin down due to its use in so many different cultural contexts. Such complexity only serves to confuse our understanding of the phenomenon itself. Yet, we can safely say that the term refers to a *constellation of magico-religious beliefs and practices* dating back to the Upper Paleolithic epoch.

The Shamanic Vocation

OF COURSE, a shaman is much 'like' a magician, and he or she is also 'like' a medicine man. Indeed, shamans are believed to be able to cure illness, like all doctors, and cast spells, like any good sorcerer. But, a shaman is much more than either. One unique title applied to the shamanic vocation by historians of religion is "psycho-pomp." That is to say, the shaman acts as guide for the spirits of the deceased into the underworld. This confirms that the shaman's principal role is that of spiritual guide, communicating with powers unseen and using this ability to better serve his or her community.

BUT above all, the shaman is a specialist in ecstatic trance. In altered states of consciousness, a shaman can fly away to visit with the 'other-than-human' powers animating this world of everyday experience. In fact, it is believed that the shaman's soul is able to leave his or her body and travel to other cosmic realms, particularly to an upper world in the heavens or into the lower regions of the underworld. This ability provides the shaman with the special status as a 'technician of the sacred'. In this respect, he or she serves as an intermediary between the seen and the unseen — healing the sick, leading souls after death, or discovering the source of larger social ills. And while the shaman has different tools to assist in achieving a state of trance — herbs, drumming, chanting, and dancing — the techniques of ecstasy have come to reside solely within his or her domain. In the final analysis, the shaman's role is restoration of balance in a world that has apparently gone off track.

Shamanism's Siberian Roots

THE ARCHEOLOGICAL record of shamanism dates back more than 30,000 years. Indeed, some of the earliest evidence of shamanic practice has been found in the Altai Region of Western Siberia, just on the north-western edge of Mongolia. So shamanism, in a real sense, may be understood as a genuine Siberian phenomenon. In fact, the word "shaman" comes from the language of the *Evenk*, a small Tungus-speaking group of hunters and reindeer herders in the Baikal region of Southern Siberia. The term is likely derived from the Pali word, *samana*, possibly from the Sanskrit *sramana*. Among the Altai people we find the word *kam* or *gam*. Similarly in the Turko-

Tartar and Mongolian tongues, *kami*. The late Mircea Eliade's work on *Shamanism* focuses in no small measure on the Altaic-Siberian roots of the phenomenon.

THE figure of the shaman represents a critical turning point in pre-history generally, and in the history of religions specifically, emerging as it does around the time of another great shift.

WITH the Pleistocene epoch giving way to the Holocene, we see major changes in both social organization and economy. There was a gradual move away from the food acquisition strategies of hunting and gathering to a more agriculturally based lifestyle including the growth of villages, the domestication of plants and animals, the emergence of urban life, and finally the eruption of political hierarchy.

THERE has been much speculation that during the Pleistocene epoch, (over one million years ago), our earliest forebears experienced a qualitatively different world than we do today. There was apparently a vital connection that our progenitors sensed with the surrounding environment. The tribe experienced the world as alive with power; there was power and sentience even in the rock, water, earth, and sky. Animism and totemism had their roots in such experience. In fact, we can still find this belief present today in the indigenous worldview throughout the Altai region and further east into Mongolia and beyond.

YET, with the Neolithic revolution, things began to change dramatically. There was a new relationship to nature developing. As farming and urbanization began to supplant hunting and gathering, the power of the untamed and nonhuman landscape no longer spoke as directly or readily to the tribe or villager. Both the natural and supernatural worlds became increasingly mute and muted by changes in technology, economy, and social organization. It is here that the shamanic vocation appeared as a lone voice where the community could still participate in those now receding powers — the shaman intervening in order to commune with the powers of nature and life.

THERE was a secret language which the shaman possessed — a means to communicate with those vital forces animating nature and effectively binding the community to its territory. This made the shaman a crucial figure within a fast changing reality, a messenger of lost mysteries and the bearer of an emergent concept of the sacred. He alone could tap into the power of a vibrant, living cosmos. His was one of the first specialized statuses in the pre-emergence of stratified society.

The Shaman's Personality

TYPICALLY, the shaman acquired his role because he manifested abnormal traits and idiosyncratic tendencies — epilepsy, sexual ambiguity, poetic sensitivity, odd dreams, or extraordinary visions calling him to his mission. As well, the role was at times assumed through heredity (passing on the family business, so to speak). But there were also rites of passage typically entailing psychological crises brought on by physical tests or isolation in a forest or desert. Shamans, in short, were required to function in two distinct but connected realms — the world of everyday experience as well as an extraordinary reality only encountered in an ecstatic journey of magical flight and visionary trance. Shamans were considered shape-shifters, changing into animal form as a helper-spirit whenever they functioned as spiritual guide or healer of their community. Indeed, in shape-shifting lay the shaman's real talent. Today, psychologists would undoubtably diagnose such individuals as schizophrenic.

WE must also realize that the shaman's peculiar status forced him or her to live as an outsider among the group he served. Physically located on the edge or outskirts of a community, he was the embodiment of "alterity" or Otherness, maintaining this social estrangement within the confines of a near sociopathic personality. There was always some level of mystery and even fear surrounding the shaman's person and her supernatural abilities. And shamans were never called upon casually, but always in more extreme need or circumstances requiring some special intervention. It must have seemed to those whom he served that the shaman existed in a social *gap*, in between what was slowly becoming the domesticated life of the villager, and his special ability to enter a separate super-sensible reality.

EVERYTHING about the shaman's wardrobe spoke of this difference. The amulets, tassels, pieces of bone, hoof, beak, fur, feather, shell, and small mirrors that adorned his costume acted as conduits of a separate reality — attracting good helping spirits while confusing or repelling the evil ones. But, it was the shaman's drum that lay at the heart of her mission, her worldview, and the ecstatic trance she would enter. It's been said that the shaman's drum, not unlike a bow, could send the shaman's soul flying into the Other world; the painted skin on the drumhead representing the shamanic cosmology — the 'World Tree' standing dead center, connecting both the upper (spiritual) and lower (earthly) realms.

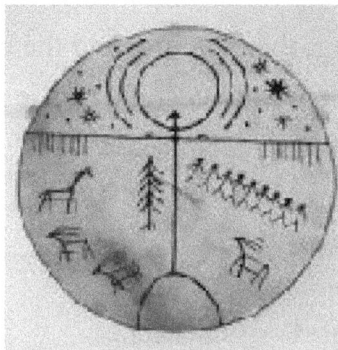

AND because the drum is believed to be made from the sacred wood of the World Tree, we can begin to understand the symbolism, the specific value, and the efficacy of its sound. We can see why, when he beats on his drum, the shaman feels himself transported in ecstatic or mystical flight to the very center of the cosmos, linking the realms and enabling communication with the awesome powers of nature. It is in such drum-induced trances that the shaman was able to fulfill his role as spiritual guide to the living as well as the dead. Yet, was the drumming, the dancing, and the chanting ALL there was to ecstatic trance and magical flight?

Magic Mushrooms

NOW, it is no secret that Siberians love
hunting for mushrooms. We might even
say that the love of mushrooms proves
their visceral attachment to Mother
Earth. Siberian shamans are no different.
They share this taste for mushrooms, and
they exercise this affinity in order to
tease open that doorway to ecstatic
trance.

AMANITA MUSCARIA or Fly Agaric
— *Muukamoor* in Russian — is the
magic mushroom, boasting a long history
as an *entheogen* (a hallucinogenic) in
Siberia as elsewhere around the world.
Muscimol, the psychoactive agent in the
mushroom, has sedative, hypnotic, and
dissociative effects. As such it can
transform one's normal sense of self —
as an ego locked in a bag of skin —
creating a genuine experience of 'being-
beside-oneself' or 'being-outside-of-
oneself,' providing the experience of
literally traversing cosmic realms. To the
Siberian shaman, the *Amanita* mushroom
was key for achieving spiritual flight —
the experience of ecstasy, a trance-like
state enabling the shaman to reach other

worlds and obtain fantastic visions. Scholars agree, it is through mushroom-induced visions that a gateway to nature's power was revealed.

Flying Reindeer?

SO WHAT do we really know about Santa Claus, I mean, Saint Nick — you know, that jolly old bearded fellow dressed in red and white, living in the North Pole and traveling by sleigh on the heels of flying reindeer delivering gifts and good tidings to all?

SIBERIAN Reindeer (*Maral*) are considered sacred animals among the indigenous tribes in many regions of Russia. Furthermore, the reindeer has been understood as a valuable helpmate by Siberian shamans throughout history. In fact, Siberian shamans often mimic the animal's appearance by donning

reindeer pelts and horns, and basically
becoming one with this spirit-helper.

AGAIN, shamans are notorious shape-
shifters in costume and in reality. As
well, they have been known to use both
the blood and urine of the reindeer in
helping them to achieve specific
'spiritual' benefits. It is no secret that
Siberian reindeer are fond of the
psychedelic *Amanita* mushroom, seeking
out this brightly colored fungus as a

quick snack under an early snowfall. For their part, shamans have been known to swallow the snow soaked with reindeer urine, thereby attaining a state of ecstatic trance while avoiding the potentially ill effects of the mushroom's poison. The sense of flight induced by imbibing this hallucinogenic-charged urine could very well account for legends of flying reindeer in our Santa fable, just as the myths describe reindeer transporting shamans to the World Tree.

IN FACT, the flying reindeer, the sleigh, and the entire foundation of our Santa mythology may have had its roots in those psychedelic, mushroom-induced, shamanic trances of Siberia where Saint Nicholas is still regarded as patron saint of travel (shamanic flight included). It may be that this Christian symbol and its iconography have simply supplanted the magical flight of the ecstatic, indigenous Siberian shaman, his dancing reindeer and their magic mushrooms.

www.ingramcontent.com/pod-product-compliance
Lightning Source LLC
Chambersburg PA
CBHW060546030426
42337CB00021B/4448